CW00864141

LOVE
YOURSELF
LOVABLE

Realising Your Authentic Loving Self Through
The Profound Yet Simple Practice Of
Ho'oponopono

LOVE

Disclaimer

This eBook is for educational purposes only, and is not intended to be a substitute for professional counselling, therapy or medical treatment. Nothing in this eBook is intended to diagnose or treat any pathology or diseased condition of the mind or body. The author will not be held responsible for any results of reading or applying the information.

Table of Contents

About Colin G Smith

For over fifteen years now I have been driven to find the very best methods of personal transformation and secrets to beneficially and magically altering our perception of reality. If you are anything like me, you're probably interested in simple and straight-forward explanations. Practical stuff that gets results! I am a NLP Master Practitioner, writer & author who has written several books including:

- How To Deal With Difficult People

- The NLP ToolBox: Your Guide Book to Neuro Linguistic Programming NLP Techniques

- Thought Symbols Magick: Manifest Your Desires in Life using the Secret Power of Sigil Magic and Thought Forms

Visit: www.amazon.com/author/colingsmith

Dedication

Dedicated to my mellifluous muse - I love you.

1. Introduction

"The PURPOSE of life is to be RESTORED BACK to LOVE, Moment by Moment." To fulfill this purpose, the individual must acknowledge that he is 100 PERCENT RESPONSIBLE for creating his life the way it is. He must come to see that it is his thoughts that create his life the way it is moment to moment. The problems are not people, places and situations but rather THE THOUGHTS OF THEM. He must come to appreciate that there is no such thing as 'out there.'" - Dr. Hew Len

If you ever ask a person directly, *"Do you love yourself?"*, more often than not you won't get a congruent positive response. But the thing is, most of the time, what we identify as *ourself*, isn't really who we are anyway. The deepest, core part of ourself, our Authentic Self, is directly connected to the Divine source of pure, unconditional love. All the other identifications we experience, such as self critic, victim, judge and so on are really just impermanent, yet repetitive, manifestations arising from *the collective subconscious database*. A useful and commonly used analogy is that our core self or Authentic Self is like the deepest depths of the ocean and the waves on the surface of the ocean are like the impermanent *subconscious database* manifestations that we get duped into identifying with. The deepest, core part of ourself then, our Authentic Self, is connected to an infinite source of unconditional love. <u>This is who we *really* are</u>, we just forget most of the time. But that's about to change as you continue reading...

Ho'oponopono

Ho - Oh - Po-no - Po-no

Ho'oponopono is a Hawaiian word meaning:

ho'o (*"to make"*) and pono (*"right"*)

On the one hand, Ho'oponopono is an incredibly simple process, yet on the other hand, as I've discovered through daily practice and research, it's also one of the most profound and elegant spiritual technologies I've ever come across. It's a problem solving method that enables you to let go and surrender to higher intelligence/source/divinity to transmute them. And the more we practice Ho'oponopono, the more we can let go of our identification with the impermanent waves, and identify more and more with the deepest depths of the ocean - our Authentic Self which is directly connected to Divinity and the source of pure, unconditional love.

"Ho'oponopono is a problem solving process of repentance, forgiveness, and transmutation that anyone can apply to themselves. It is a process of petitioning Divinity to convert error memories in the Unihipili (Lower Self) to zero, to nothing." - Dr. Hew Len

Join me now as we dip into the history of this fascinating practice...

Morrnah Nalamaku Simeona

A gifted healer from Hawaii, a woman named Morrnah

Nalamaku Simeona, who was also a native Kahuna, transformed an ancient spiritual tradition into an efficient modern healing method. To show appreciation towards her achievements, the Hawaiians refered to Morrnah as, *"a Living Treasure of Hawaii,"* because what she did impacted life in a way no one thought possible. Let us take a look at her story, to better understand why this woman was so outstanding.

She was born in a special and respected family, in Honolulu, on the 19th of May 1913. It is probably her mother that passed on the gift of healing, as she was among the few Kahuna Lapa'au kahea; a person that uses the power of chants and words in the healing process. Lilia Simeona was a highly appreciated woman, being the personal assistant of Queen Lili'uokalani towards the end of her life, as she was the last queen that reigned in Hawaii. The Hawaiian word, *"Kahuna,"* has various meanings. The people that are given this title could also be known as a shaman, priest/priestess, or magician. Taking into account the activity of a Kahuna, we can say that this person has the role of a traditional shaman, being the spiritual leader of the community, creating a middle ground between the seen and unseen world, keeping them in balance.

As mentioned before, Morrnah was born into a family where she was surrounded by healing through words and chants. So it was just a matter of time until she started practicing this form of healing as well. For her, the presence of outer and inner worlds was common, being able to sense the energies flowing from one world to another. She was only three years old when her family noticed that Morrnah had inherited the talents of her mother. The training to become a Kahuna is not easy, because all the knowledge is transmitted orally, as there are no books to read or notes to take into account. The person that started this training had to have natural abilities to remember the things that were taught by the teacher, as everything was transmitted through the power of words. And if this was not enough, the training was intensive, as there was little time for it to be done, the teacher repeating twice, or three times at the most, the information the student needed to learn. So those who couldn't keep up the pace were left behind by the teachers, as they chose not to invest their time and effort in the ones that were not gifted with a good memory.

Along with the traditional Hawaiian spiritual teachings, Morrnah also attended courses in a Catholic school, absorbing the teachings of Jesus Christ which influenced her path. But, she did live in the way her parents and ancestors did, practicing the traditional method of healing and being a respected member of the community. For Hawaiians, the Kahuna was a very important part of the community, being involved in almost every aspect of local life. If an illness did not responded to a variety of treatments, like herbal medicine, massages or healing through chanting, it was considered that the disease was produced by an unbalance in the entire community. Thus, a Ho'oponopono healing was necessary in these cases, meaning a *"family healing."*

Morrnah also performed lomi lomi, which is the Hawaiian healing massage, being a master in this practice as well. Touching the body while performing the healing massage, her ability to sense the energetic flow in the organism could also help her know where something was wrong with the health of a person; she used this ability to balance the energy within a person's body. Using her talent, Morrnah had spas at the Kahala Hilton hotel and the Royal Hawaiian hotel, performing healing sessions through massage and energy-work. Slowly, people from Western society started to discover Hawaii with the help of these spas. During her long activity, Morrnah ended up treating personalities like Jackie Kennedy and Arnold Palmer. These encounters made Morrnah see that people coming from Western culture were generally out of balance because they couldn't connect their spirit with the *"Higher Beings,"* as she would say, because they had reached the extremes of intellectuality, forgetting how to let energy flow naturally through themselves.

She also knew that Ho'oponopono, the *"family healing,"* could help the pain and disease Morrnah found in Western people. The main purpose of this practice, is that during the process, an error is corrected, restoring peace and balance. The entire family needs to take part in it, a facilitator supporting the healing process, while each member of the family asks for forgiveness from the rest of the members. Still, she also knew that such a thing was hard to achieve in a Western family, as they were scattered and dismantled, making the healing process very hard to put together. So, in 1976, at the age of 63, Morrnah started to develop a new type of Ho'oponopono, changing the traditional form and adapting it to the needs of modern society.

Dr. Ihaleakala Hew Len

Dr. Ihaleakala Hew Len is a master healer in the art of Ho'oponopono. As a Hawaiian native, Hew Len spent many years studying self enlightenment and the power of Ho'oponopono made popular by iconic healer Morrnah Simeone.

Simeone healed Dr. Hew Len's daughter using the healing power of Ho'oponopono; she suffered from shingles for over ten years without any success of treatment. Upon witnessing Simeone's success with healing his daughter, he immediately began studying under Simeone and has been practicing the ancient healing art since 1982. Throughout his eighty plus years on Earth, he has accomplished a wide myriad of tasks in the realm of healing and wellness.

From 1984 to 1987, while working at Hawaii State Hospital Kaneohe, Hew Len *cleaned* a full high security wing of psychiatric patients, many of whom needed to be physically restrained. *"The violence stopped"*, as Hew Len states, and three years later, a majority of the patients were released from the ward as a result of his work. This miraculous happening formed a following for Dr. Hew Len, opening the eyes of healers and students throughout the world. (You can read a full article about this incredible event
at: http://www.mrfire.com/article-archives/new-articles/worlds-most-unusual-therapist.html)

Dr. Hew Len is the president and administrator of the Foundation of I, Inc in Hawaii and, in association with the foundation, worked with the United Nations, UNESCO, the International Human Unity Conference on World Peace,

Traditional Indian Medicine Conference, Healers for Peace and others to bring enlightenment and peace to the wounded communities of today.

His healings through Ho'oponopono have become known throughout the world and, in result, Dr. Hew Len has offered his services in the forms of workshops, clinics and literature. He wrote, *"Zero Limits,"* along with Dr. Joe Vitale which takes the reader on the journey of reaching a state of being known as, *"zero,"* where a person is able to cleanse negativity and form a connection with the Divine.

In terms familiar to our modern world, Hew Len refers to the negativity we build up throughout our lives as *"data"* and he refers to himself as a *"cleaner."* He cleanses negative data that he shares with patients to heal the thoughts and previous *"negative programming"* as passed on from ancestors going back to the beginning of time.

Dr. Joe Vitale

Dr. Joe Vitale, commonly known as, *"the Buddha of the Internet,"* is an author of self-help books focused on positive thinking and the Law of Attraction (LOA). He was born in Niles, Ohio on December 29th, 1953 and received his education from Kent University and Belford University with a focus on Metaphysics. The good doctor is certified in hypnotherapy and practices healing through Chun Kung.

His charismatic personality and positive outlook on life turned around his life in the 1970s, when he suffered from the loss of his job and home. Instead of self-pity, Vitale employed positive thinking and grew to be the marketing success that is he today.

Dr. Vitale published his first self-help book in 1984 which focused on the Law of Attraction and how thinking positive thoughts will lead to positive things in return. The Attractor Factor, Zero Limits and Attract Money Now are examples of published works – one of which Zero Limits being co-written by iconic Hawaiian healer Dr. Hew Len. He writes his books passionately and quickly – usually within three weeks! He has over ten motivational books currently on the market ranging from marketing advice to hypnotic writing techniques.

Along with writing, Dr. Vitale enjoys acting and has starred in movies such as The Secret, TV shows like Donny Deutsch's and even made an appearance on Larry King Live with his healing methods appearing on NBC and Oprah. Joe is also an award winning musician with songs nominated for the Posi Awards. His four albums feature songs about positive thinking and its life changing effects which has coined him the title: *"First Self-Help Singer and Songwriter."*

The theme of positive thinking follows Joe everywhere he goes as he travels to help others. For twenty five years he has offered methods of making money, being successful and basic self-improvement. He founded the Attract Miracles Community which strives to improve the world by practicing self-improvement. His methods of success involve *"cleaning"* and *"clearing"* utilising the practice of Ho'oponopono to become awakened, and then using this awakened state to find success in life.

Self Identity Through Ho'oponopono

"Divine creator, father, mother, son as one. If I, my family, relatives, and ancestors have offended you, your family, relatives, and ancestors in thoughts, words, deeds, and actions from the beginning of our creation to the present, we ask your forgiveness. Let this cleanse, purify, release, cut all the negative memories, blocks, energies, and vibrations and transmute these unwanted energies to pure light. And it is done." - Morrnah Nalamaku Simeona

So, as mentioned earlier, Morrnah Simeona realised that a new form of Ho'oponopono was needed in order to help modern day people derive benefit from it. In her new method known as, *Self Identity Through Ho'oponopono*, which is what most people now know of as simply, *"Ho'oponopono,"* the transformation happens between the person and Divinity. To transmute problems, a person directs the following sentences to divinity: *"I love you / I'm sorry / Please forgive me / Thank you."* It doesn't matter in what order these sentences are said, as long as they are said over and over again like reciting a mantra. By doing so, we can surrender to the divine source of unconditional love, let go of our intellectual ego grasping, and allow divinity to transmute our problems instead - leading to more peace and freedom. And the more we practice this simple method, the more we can get a taste of our Authentic Self Identity which is connected to the Source of Unconditional Love.

2. Spiritual Technology

Spiritual Technology

"Cease trying to work everything out with your minds. It will get you nowhere. Live by intuition and inspiration and let your whole life be Revelation." - Eileen Caddy

In this section you will be introduced to the *Spiritual Technology* of Ho'oponopono that will enable you to realise your authentic loving self while becoming more loving of others. The methodology is based around a few fundamental concepts that we will now explore.

Total Responsibility or 100% Responsibility

Isn't it easier to blame others for the problems that appear in our life? Whenever something is not working right, we will often try to find excuses and place the blame on others. But, does this make us mature and responsible? Well, not exactly, because not taking responsibility for our choices, deeds and everything that happens in our life, is a cop-out. Taking full responsibility for your thoughts and actions may not be the easiest task, because some situations in life can be very challenging. But taking personal responsibility is not a burden, because in reality it will help you develop your strength of character and will help you make better decisions.

You must be aware of the fact that you are the only one responsible for the thoughts and actions that you make in your lifetime, and not others. You choose the path you walk in life, and you can't really blame others for what is happening to you or for the choices you have made. Personal responsibility also involves being your own best friend; having the ability to be able to support, love and encourage yourself. It's also about being able to be honest with yourself concerning the abilities, skills, knowledge and weaknesses you have, and what can be done to improve them.

Taking personal responsibility will help you lead a better life. How? By acknowledging that you are the only one that influences everything that appears in your life; you are the one making the decisions and choices throughout your life, day-to-day. You should not be afraid of making mistakes or failing, because this is part of the learning and development process. If you do something wrong, accept the fact that you were wrong, and move on, making amends for your mistake in the best way you can, after acquiring the knowledge that will help you do that.

Taking responsibility for your thoughts, decisions and actions means that you have accepted life as a mature person. In time, this will make you stronger, more secure in your decision making skills, and wiser. Only through experiences, both good and bad, do we begin to master ourselves. So find the courage within yourself to take full responsibility for what you do, say and choose.

Ho'oponopono teaches us that to transform our lives and become more loving, we need to take **Total Responsibility** and practice transforming the problems that appear to us. The idea is that whatever we perceive or experience in our

Universe, we take responsibility for it appearing to us; the understanding is that there is something within ourselves that co-creates our experience of reality. More often than not, we try to push problems away in a state of non-acceptance, but unfortunately this approach tends to get poor results, like the old adage says, *"resistance causes persistence."*

Interconnectedness

We are used to thinking about ourselves as individual entities, and are under the illusion that everything that happens around us, occurs independently and separately from us. But according to some of the oldest spiritual philosophies in the world, nothing exists in isolation because everything is interconnected. What happens takes place because of the existent relationships between the elements of the Universe, and not as isolated spontaneous events. Practically, everything that exists in this world, creatures, people and things are all manifest due to certain causes and conditions.

Interconnectedness is based on the fact that the existence of a thing depends on the existence of another thing, and vice versa. None of the two things would exist if one of them was removed or disappeared. Everything is organised like a well connected chain, with things going out of balance if one of the rings of this chain is removed. Even our entire life is based on internal and external relationships with certain factors. All the details that make-up our life, such as our personality, choices, experiences, and also the things that happen on the outside, are influenced by the existence of these relationships. All of us contribute in one way or another to the unfolding of the Universe, influencing the existence of all the other things that appear in it. Thus, we all live and exist in a holistic manner, where every aspect is in connection with another one, creating a huge interconnected web. When we understand this, we will also realise that selfishness and critical thoughts about others will not lead to happiness.

Some spiritual traditions state that the family we are born into is not a random event, as we start our life there in order to learn certain lessons and perfect ourselves as we advance in life. We lose precious time in quarrels with others, in victimising ourselves and in trying to express vengeance, wondering why our life does not become better. We end up living a bitter life blaming our parents for our failures, envying our friends and neighbours for their accomplishments, regretting the decisions we've made in our own lives and feeling sorry for not having what they have. If we are not aware of the fact that everything is interconnected and the way that this influences our lives, we will not be able to have the life we really desire.

The concept of Total Responsibility goes beyond what *you* say, do, and think; <u>it even includes what *others* say, do, and think!</u> Yes it's quite radical. Taking on this special point of view, means we stop blaming anyone or anything for our current experience of reality. It's not your fault but it is your responsibility to accept the problems you're presented with and transform them through proven transmutation methods such as Ho'oponopono.

19

Taking Total Responsibility for everything that appears in your Universe is a tall order but it's also really empowering. It means you can't blame anyone or anything for undesirable circumstances, and it places you in control of your own thoughts, feelings and perceptions. Total Responsibility is best experienced as being part of a daily spiritual practice that you have to continually remind yourself of because it's so antithesis to conventional societies, *"culture of blame."*

I've personally found it takes a lot of effort to adopt this mind-set, even after many months of daily practice; the inner child will shout and scream in an attempt to shirk responsibility. But when I do, I feel much more congruent within myself as an adult human being and it feels empowering.

"It's not your fault but it is your responsibility." - Joe Vitale

(What this phrase really means is: *"It's not your fault but it is your responsibility to transform the problems that appear in your Universe."*)

The Three Selves

The three selves model of the human being is a very robust one that has a long history and is taught in many spiritual traditions throughout the world. On first viewing it can appear quite simplistic, yet it is actually a very elegant and profound model of the way human consciousness functions.

Your Higher Self (Authentic Self)

Synonyms: Soul, Super-Consciousness, Essential/Real/Authentic/True/Divine Self, Atman, Parental Guardian Spirit, Higher Consciousness, Aumakua (Hawaiian)

"You cannot be denied anything that is perfect, whole, complete, and right for you when you are your Self first. Being your Self first you automatically experience perfection in the way of Divine Thoughts, Words, Deeds, and Actions. Allowing your toxic thoughts to be first, you automatically experience imperfection in the way of disease, confusion, resentment, depression, judgement, and poverty." - Dr. Hew Len

Your Higher Self or Authentic Self is the part of you that has been around since *beginningless time* and is immortal and at one with Divinity - the source of unconditional love. Using another synonym, Parental Guardian Spirit, can help us understand how this part of ourselves has unconditional love for us and can wisely guide our direction in life <u>when we ask</u>. But one of the problems we experience, as humans, is that the Lower Self blocks the connection to the Higher Self and the flow of unconditional love. This is due to our own life memories and the thought-forms or *programs* stored in the vast collective sub-conscious *database*; they manifest as thoughts, emotions and body sensations generated in the Lower Self.

Your Middle Self (Conscious Mind)

Synonyms: Ego, I, Me, Intellect, Conscious Self, Uhane

(Hawaiian)

This is the part of ourselves that we are most familiar with. It is our, "I." It is the logical, rational part of ourselves. *"I think... I am... I do... I have..."* We can do amazing things with this intelligence; design houses, write novels, create works of art, write music, philosophise, create businesses and so on. But the conscious mind has a very limited span of awareness; vast amounts of data coming into the senses are filtered out. This part of ourself expresses it's power most effectively when focusing on goals and specificities. But the main purpose of the Middle Self is the ability to choose and make decisions. Dr. Hew Len is found of saying, *"you can either choose to have incessant memories replaying or you can choose to do incessant Cleaning (Ho'oponopono.)"*

Your Lower Self (Subconscious Mind)

Synonyms: Inner Child, Unconscious Self, Unihipili (Hawaiian)

This part of ourself takes care of some very important, life sustaining functions such as; making our heart beat, making the lymph system circulate, making our breathing function, making the digestion system work and many other essential automatic bodily functions. The Lower Self is responsible for generating our emotions and body sensations and we can also call this part, *our Inner Child*. All of the subconscious memories from this life and previous lives are stored in this part of ourself. And it goes much deeper than that: We are also connected into a **collective** storehouse of memories.

The Collective Storehouse Consciousness (Alayavijnana)

"We are the sum total of our experiences, which is to say that we are burdened by our pasts. When we experience stress or fear in our lives, if we would look carefully, we would find that the cause is actually a memory. It is the emotions which are tied to these memories which affect us now. The subconscious associates an action or person in the present with something that happened in the past. When this occurs, emotions are activated and stress is produced." - Morrnah Nalamaku Simeona

According to Mahayana Buddhism we are all influenced by something known as the Alayavijnana (a Sanskrit term meaning, *"collective storehouse consciousness."*) This pre-dates Jung's, Collective Unconscious, by thousands of years and offers a more accurate understanding. It is seen as a container that has accumulated karma from out past actions and experiences. If we translate the word "alaya" from Sanskrit, it means "basis" or "foundation."

In the Mahayana philosophy, alayavijnana represents the eighth level from a total of eight levels of Yogacara (*practice of yoga*), the sector that is concerned with what we accumulate through our experiences. It makes reference to the awareness that connects something facultative with something objective, such as the eyes with the image. The alayavijnana composes the basis of our personality, because it contains the primary forms of our thoughts, desires, opinions, and attachments that have developed through our numerous incarnations from *beginningless time*. It also contains the primordial forms, or seeds, of our karma. Karma is triggered by our acts and intentions, whether they are done through deeds, words, or thoughts. So, it slowly grows at a subconscious level, until it becomes fully ripened, or until it is eliminated through purification methods.

The alayavijnana should not be considered as being a self, because it is just a large collection of the attributes that compose a self, so it is not the self itself. A similarity with the western subconscious mind concept is the fact that this storehouse consciousness is capable of influencing the way we experience our life and the actions we do. Our perception of the things that appear to us are influenced by this storehouse consciousness as well; it contains emotional traits, beliefs and other *"filters."* This is why we all see things so differently, even if we may be looking at the same object at the same time. So basically our perception, in the here and now, is influenced by the experiences we have accumulated during many lifetimes, collected in this *storehouse consciousness.*

However we can keep things simple and realise that basically there are millions upon millions of thought-forms stored in the alayavijnana and they are bubbling up and flowing through us the vast majority of the time.

It may help our understanding by using modern day Information Technology terminology: We have memories, data, or programs that are stored in a *database* within the collective sub-conscious mind. We are all connected to this and therefore share *programs* with other people. So when we, for example, have the experience of someone being angry at us, that *data* or *program* is a shared one and so it is also within us. By taking 100% responsibility and practicing Ho'oponopono we are given the opportunity to clear/clean/void the *problem data* from ourselves, the other person, and the collective *database*.

Non-Dualism

There are different philosophical schools about non-dualism or non-duality. Personally I prefer the Madhyamaka view about the non-duality of conventional and ultimate truth: All phenomena, everything we experience in our perception of reality, all objects, all forms we perceive, are in actuality empty of inherent existence; they don't exist from their own side. Conventionally things exist but ultimately everything is empty of inherent existence. This knowledge is encapsulated in Buddha's incredibly succinct statement: *"Form is emptiness. Emptiness is form."*

The problem for us is that thought-forms bubble up from the Alayavijnana (*Subconscious Database*) and enter our sub-conscious mind as memories, feelings, beliefs and so on, and these filter our perception of phenomena and we get tricked into thinking that is reality. Dr. Hew Len is fond of using a whiteboard to help clarify our understanding: The pure, clean whiteboard is our Authentic Self. He then writes a letter 'M' in the middle of the board that symbolises how we get tricked into identifying with Memories rather then identifying with our pure, clean Self - the whiteboard. The good news is that we don't really need to understand complex philosophies

25

about the nature of reality to transform our lives, we just need to practice a straight-forward and proven method like Ho'oponopono.

Surrendering, Letting Go And Transmutation

"We can appeal to Divinity who knows our personal blueprint, for healing all thoughts and memories that are holding us back at this time." - Morrnah Nalamaku Simeona

Ho'oponopono is essentially a *surrendering process*; it's about letting go, or releasing our subconscious thought-forms (patterns/programs/beliefs/memories) **by surrendering and allowing Divinity to purify/transmute them**. Doing so enables us to connect back into *The Source* of pure potentiality, through the antahkarana (a Sanskrit word meaning *"Rainbow Bridge"*) connection with our Higher Self or Soul. This gives rise to a genuinely creative behavioural response instead of the usual robotic response. And the fact is, most of the time we are mainly functioning like robots in, *"the deep sleep of ignorance,"* as Buddha said. Our Conscious Mind or intellect likes to think it understands what's happening but really it is rather clueless; reality is far too vast and complex! Only Divinity really knows what's going on.

So, using an example to clarify, let's say we have the experience of someone being angry with us: Using this special mind-set, we would take 100% responsibility and accept that <u>we</u> have, *"stuff in the subconscious database,"* that we need to let go of. And, let's remember, our conscious ego mind's awareness is incredibly myopic. It likes to have a go at interpreting what is going on, but we can't really understand what is happening in reality; it is far to complex, and the good news is, we don't need to know. So enjoy practicing letting go and allowing the Divine Source to purify and transmute the erroneous thought-forms instead.

The Story Of The Chinese Farmer

- Alan Watts

Once upon a time there was a Chinese farmer, whose horse ran away. All the neighbours came around to commensurate that evening, *"So sorry to hear your horse has ran away. That's too bad."* And he said, *"Maybe."*

The next day the horse came back, bringing seven wild horses with it, and everybody came around in the evening and said, *"Oh, isn't that lucky. What a great turn of events. You've now got eight horses."* And he said, *"Maybe."*

The next day his son tried to break one of these horses and ride it and was thrown and broke his leg. And they all said, *"Oh, dear that's too bad."* And he said, *"Maybe."*

The following day the conscription officers came around to recruit to force people into the army and they rejected his son, because he had a broken leg. And all the people came around and said, *"Isn't that great."* And he said, *"Maybe."*

You see that is the attitude of not thinking of things in terms of gain or loss, advantage or disadvantage, because you don't really know. The fact that you might get a letter from a solicitor, I mean from a law office tomorrow, saying that some distant relative of yours has left you a million dollars, it might be something you would feel very, very happy about, but the disasters that it could lead to are unbelievable. Internal Revenue – to mention only one part of that.

So you never really know whether something is fortune or misfortune.

The Four Phrase Ho'oponopono Mantra

A mantra is the arrangement of words or syllables that are chanted in a repetitive fashion as part of religious or spiritual ritual. *Mantra*, meaning sound, is deemed as a sacred utterance or syllable. More than 3,000 years old, the practice of mantras have their beginnings in India and continue to be an important aspect of Hindu and Buddhist religious ceremonies or rites. The syllable *om* is a very popular mantra in Hinduism with the principle mantra in Buddhism being, *"om mani padme hum."*

Mantras may be used as religious worship, spiritual evolution, purification or they can be used to clear one's mind, promote natural healing and induce relaxation. Mantras help the mind stay centred in the present moment. While many traditional mantra's use Sanskrit words for a specific desired outcome, it can also be as simple as choosing a word or sentence that is soothing and repeating it over and over again to induce a positive mindset.

The thing to remember is that there are different types of mantras that can stimulate various states of consciousness. Experts will say that you should take them seriously because the inappropriate use of mantras could have the opposite effect of what is actually desired. However, when used correctly, mantras can prove to be magical in the sense that they can raise your level of consciousness.

In recent years, Mantra meditation has increased in popularity. Mantra meditations may be used during meditation to create an induced trance-like state, leading the meditator to a higher level of spiritual awareness. Mantra meditation also has a positive effect on health including but not limited to the following:

1. Lower blood pressure

2. Lower heart rate

3. Reduced risk for depression and anxiety

4. Improved relaxation and wellness

Chanting mantras can create positive changes and lead to deeper states of meditation as a result of the subtle vibrations. Studies have shown that people who regularly chant mantras demonstrate better coping skills than those who do not. Mantra chanting may be done by an individual or in a group setting enabling chanters to focus on the unity of the voices and vibrations.

Ho'oponopono practice involves reciting a simple four line English language mantra:

"I love you"
"I'm sorry"
"Please forgive me"
"Thank you"

You can choose to say the mantra out loud or just in your head and it isn't necessary to say each line emphatically. The most important thing is to simply repeat the mantra again and again to get the best results from this practice. Each part of the mantra will now be explained in more detail below:

"I Love You" (Love)

"Our illusion of separation from Love is the root of all our suffering." - DeNoyelles

"I love you" is probably the most powerful phrase in the English language and the term is known in all languages in the world. You can say this to yourself, other people, your thoughts, animals, plants, beings in other realms, and material objects such as buildings.

When you repeat this phrase in the Ho'oponopono process, it helps you connect with the state of consciousness known as love, cultivates greater self acceptance and connects you with your own *inner divinity*. In fact, probably the best way to harness the power of the phrase, *"I love you,"* is to address it to the Divine. Doing so will help you establish a stronger connection to your own Higher Self which is at one with the pure source of Divinity/Unconditional Love. And because Ho'oponopono is ultimately a surrendering and petitioning process to the Divine, practicing it this way will help you learn this indispensable skill.

"I'm Sorry" (Repentance)

This phrase also contains a lot of power in it. Have you ever had the experience of giving someone a sincere apology or have you ever received a sincere apology from someone? It opens your heart up a little because there is love contained within it.

With the Ho'oponopono method when we say, *"I'm sorry,"* we are acknowledging that the problems that are appearing to us are due to the *erroneous subconscious database programs* in our lower self, and we are sorry that basically we are asleep and unaware.

"Please Forgive Me" (Forgiveness)

"You don't say, 'please forgive me' to the Divine because the Divine needs to hear it; you say it because you need to hear it." - Dr. Hew Len

This is really about forgiving yourself for being in the, *"deep sleep of ignorance."* It's not about feeling guilty, it's about <u>accepting</u> that you are ignorant and have made mistakes due to being influenced by *data* in the *subconscious database.* The phrases, *"I'm sorry"* and, *"please forgive me,"* also acknowledge the significant fact that you are willing to take responsibility to make amends. The modern Ho'oponopono method is always about forgiving yourself, it's not about forgiving others; if we remember the Total Responsibility principle, the process is all about acknowledging and accepting that everything that appears to us, including the perception of *problem people*, is co-created by us; it's simply an error within ourselves that creates the experience we are having. Repeating the phrase, *"please forgive me,"* together with the other Ho'oponopono phrases, helps us achieve greater inner peace within ourself.

"Thank You" (Gratitude)

By repeating the phrase, *"thank you,"* you are tuning in to the state of consciousness known as gratitude. This is a very powerful state of being, which has similarities to love. You can address this phrase to yourself, other people, your thoughts, your inner child, or the Universe. However probably the best way, as mentioned above with the, *"I love you,"* statement, is to address the phrase to the Divine. Expressing gratitude to the Divine Source of Unconditional Love is a very powerful thing to practice and it helps you remember your own Divine essence.

3. Love Yourself Loveable

Daily Spiritual Practice

"The PURPOSE of life is to be RESTORED BACK to LOVE, Moment by Moment." To fulfill this purpose, the individual must acknowledge that he is 100 PERCENT RESPONSIBLE for creating his life the way it is. He must come to see that it is his thoughts that create his life the way it is moment to moment. The problems are not people, places and situations but rather THE THOUGHTS OF THEM. He must come to appreciate that there is no such thing as 'out there.'" - Dr. Hew Len

As I mentioned in the introduction of this book, Ho'oponopono, on the one hand, is a very simple process which is essentially based around repeating the four line mantra:

"I love you"
"I'm sorry"
"Please forgive me"
"Thank you"

But, as you'll discover, the more you practice Ho'oponopono, the more you'll realise it's profound depths; in fact the main purpose of Ho'oponopono is to become increasingly familiar with your Authentic Self. There are no strict rules about how you should practice this method; for example you can repeat the mantra statements in any order you prefer. However it's been found that addressing **all of the mantra** statements to Divinity provides the best results; this also helps you establish a stronger connection with your own Divine essence through familiarity and repetition.

All of the problems we experience in life can be an opportunity to let go/release/clean/purify and transmute, while becoming more familiar with our Authentic Self that is connected to divinity. Remember the old adage, *"resistance causes persistence."* Resisting taking responsibility is like one hand pushing against the other, rather than loving the *enemy* (problem) and releasing it into the Divine void.

Another way of looking at this purification or cleaning process is that you are removing the poison (subconscious memories/programs) from within yourself. A wonderful analogy, comes from the animal kingdom: Peacocks thrive on poisonous plants. They will even eat small poisonous snakes if they are colourful enough! It is said that their plumage is made more colourful by the plants, flowers and insects they eat. So enjoy transforming the problems that appear to you and notice yourself becoming more alive and colourful.

Ho'oponopono is a genuine spiritual practice for modern times. Many people are too busy to meditate properly but with this practice you can sit and concentrate on specific issues for a few minutes at a time, or you can walk around with your eyes open repeating the mantra. In fact you can make it become your internal dialogue even while doing various mundane tasks with a bit of practice. This proven method provides us with an incredible opportunity to purify our mind-stream while connecting to our own Divine source within, 24 hours a day if we so choose...

Ho'oponopono Methods

1. Specific Problems

The most powerful way to practice Ho'oponopono is on specific problems. You start off by thinking about what the problem is that you want to solve. e.g.) *"I find my boss really annoying,"* or, *"I hate myself,"* or, *"She's so angry!"*

Next you take 100% responsibility by accepting that there is something within yourself that is co-creating the problem: You ask the question, *"What is it within myself that I need to let go of?"* More often than not there will be a certain feeling or sensation in your body. That is good enough to run with because this is not about analysing. Remember Ho'oponopono is a process of surrendering to Divinity to transmute our problems: So we ask the question, get a small sense of what it is within ourself, and then allow the Divine to do it's transmutation magic by repeating the mantra.

When you get started with this approach, at first aim to do just 5 minutes sitting down. I suggest you use a timer as well because it can be surprising how you can fool yourself into thinking you've done 5 minutes when in fact you've only done 3 minutes. Once you've got used to doing 5 minutes of mantra recitation, you can move on to 10 minutes. It's very beneficial to keep a record of what you have been practicing on so you can understand what progress you have been making and where you need to do more *cleaning.* Take a look at the short section titled, *"How To Keep A Practice Diary,"* coming up soon in this chapter.

2. Before Events

Another very beneficial practice is to do Ho'oponopono before you go into a situation. For example fifteen minutes before you are to go into work or meet a business colleague, tune in to yourself, take 100% responsibility and ask yourself, *"What is it within myself that I need to let go of?"* You then proceed to recite the mantra for 5/10/20 minutes. Remember that subconscious memories/programs are constantly arising from the *collective subconscious database*, and when you interact with other people, shared memories/programs will get triggered, so doing some *clearing* beforehand is a very good practice.

3. Continuous Mantra

Ideally we want to be performing Ho'oponopono ALL THE TIME! The mantra will have become our constant *internal dialogue*, meaning we would be cleaning errors in the subconscious database, consistently, while connecting to our Divine Source - all the time. However it will take some practice because of life's demands. But we can make a good start by repeating the mantra when driving, washing up, cleaning, cooking and when performing other mundane tasks. Another excellent time to practice Ho'oponopono is when you go to bed at night. When you wake up in the morning automatically repeating the mantra, you are making good progress.

Top Tip 1: All of the above methods can be done for longer periods, and more comfortably, by taking a walk. Start off with 100% responsibility: Ask yourself, *"What do I need to let go of* *within myself?"* And then simply go for a 20 minute or longer walk while repeating the mantra.

Top Tip 2: When performing Ho'oponopono you may get glimpses of the shared memories in your subconscious, but it's good to remember that this special process isn't about analysing and grasping, it's a practice of letting go and allowing Divine intelligence to do the work.

Top Tip 3: You can streamline the mantra by removing the line, *"I'm sorry,"* and then just repeat the other three statements: *"I love you,"* *"Please forgive me,"* *"Thank you."* According to Dr. Hew Len you can even just use the following two line mantra and get beneficial results: *"I love you,"* *"Thank you."*

The Mirror Exercise

The standard mirror exercise is a fairly well known method for improving self acceptance and self esteem. It is recommended that you do this exercise every day for 21 days and notice how it's changed your life. The exercise is best done in a quiet private place when you are relaxed and in front of a full length mirror. You simply look into your eyes in the mirror for about five minutes. Start off by just looking at yourself, while initially this may feel uncomfortable it is a vital part of the exercise. After a few seconds begin to look at your eyes, your skin and your body. The standard approach is to say nice things to yourself such as, *"you are beautiful,"* but the exercise is enhanced considerably by repeating the Ho'oponopono mantra to yourself, either out loud or silently to yourself.

Many people in modern society have a lot of *negative programming*, especially around their self concept or self image. Doing the mirror exercise, combined with Ho'oponopono, every day will help you draw out the subconscious thought-forms that are affecting your self image, ready for transmutation, leading to greater self acceptance. So give this 5 minute exercise a go every day for the next 21 days and you may be surprised how much more esteemed you feel about yourself and others.

Ho'oponopono Examples

Example 1: Annoying Work Colleagues

I once started working in a new job and I found one of the men in the department domineering and even a bit of a bully. After a few weeks of putting up with his snide and passive-aggressive comments, I noticed myself becoming increasingly angry, to the point where I was having thoughts about hitting him. I realised I better do something about it. The ordinary response would be to just think he is an annoying person and have critical thoughts about him. But using the principle of Total Responsibility we would accept the reality of what we are experiencing, keeping in mind that it is really the shared memories and *programs* in the sub-conscious *database* that creates the experience we are having. It is this *data*, in the sub-conscious mind, with which we practice the cleaning/clearing/purifying tools of Ho'oponopono in order to transform the problem *data*, allowing love and inspiration to flow into our being instead of the old sub-conscious *programs*.

I sat down and thought about this *domineering person* and noticed my feelings about the situation. I then asked myself, *"what is it within myself that I need to let go of?"* I then proceeded to do Ho'oponopono by repeating the mantra for 10 minutes. Afterwards I felt slightly calmer but I knew I had more *clearing* to do. I got on with doing other things but the next day I did another 10 minutes of Ho'oponopono and afterwards I felt that something had shifted in my energy field with regards to the relationship dynamic. Now the most interesting part is that later on during the same day I bumped into this man by chance and after a brief, *"the weather is nice today"* chat, the conversation, some how, led to him revealing that his Dad had died when he was a teenager and it had deeply affected him. On learning of this, my whole perception of him shifted and I felt more open hearted and warmer towards the human being in front of me. Apart from me deciding to take responsibility and spend a total of twenty minutes reciting mantra's, no will power was used to, *"get better rapport,"* the *healing* came about spontaneously. My relationship with this man has been better ever since.

Example 2: Money Problems

I got a notification from Amazon saying I needed to update my IRS Tax information. When I started filling in the form it said my unique tax number was incorrect and I couldn't fill in the form. I found this very stressful because if I couldn't fill in the form it would mean I would get taxed 30% of my royalties. I felt victimised and angry at the IRS for being able to extract money from me, even though I don't even live in the USA. I believe my strong feelings were exaggerated due to the many thought-forms there must be in the *collective subconscious database* with regards to the IRS. I don't really know if that's true or not but I took 100% responsibility, noticed my feelings of fear and anger, and asked myself, *"what is it within myself that I need to let go of?"* I then proceeded to do Ho'oponopono by repeating the mantra for about 20 minutes and felt calmer afterwards. The next day I decided to have another look at the form, feeling much calmer, and was surprised to notice a little tick box that I hadn't seen previously that allowed me to use my UK Tax number instead.

Example 3: Why Is She So Angry With Me?!

I had the experience with a women in that most of the time she seemed to be really angry or irritated with me and I hadn't done anything to provoke this anger as far as I could tell. Most of the time when I spoke to her she seemed to be tense and irritated and would often snap at me for no good reason. Admittedly it took a while but I finally decided to take Total Responsibility and asked myself, *"what is it within myself that I need to let go of?"* and started applying Ho'opnopono. After a while I did start perceiving some glimpses of what it was within myself that was co-creating the experience I was having with this woman; it seemed I had many childhood memories, mainly of resentment towards my mother, and to a lesser extent, towards my sister. I spent many hours over days and weeks clearing these subconscious memories. It's important to note that I didn't grasp and analyse any of those memories because one of the wonderful things about Ho'oponopono is that it is a practice of letting go; allowing Divinity to transmute our problems. The only conscious effort we need to make is taking 100% Responsibility and reciting the mantra.

After many hours (*over several days*) of Ho'oponopono practice, it became apparent to me that the problem I was experiencing with this woman was way beyond my unresolved subconscious childhood resentments being projected outwards, it was much deeper: Shared previous life issues? Ancestral memories? Her stuff? Who really knows? But I'm inclined to agree with Dr. Hew Len: After decades of practicing Ho'oponopono he states that there is a massive field of distrust between men and women within the collective subconscious database. To me this makes sense; humanity has been living with extreme violence in all it's grotesque forms for thousands of years. And unfortunately much of the violence has been committed against women.

So both men and women have within their subconscious database, millions of memories and programs of distrust deriving from the so called, *"battle of the sexes,"* which has been going on for centuries. Currently we also have an increasing culture of infidelity and higher divorce rates than ever before. This is a painful and tragic consequence of modern culture that plunges many people into states of despair with regards to experiencing a trusting, loving relationship. However, the good news is that by taking 100%

Responsibility and practicing Ho'oponopono we can, man or woman, begin cleaning up this collective *data of violence and distrust.*

Example 4: Negative Thoughts About Yourself

Many people experience negative thoughts about themselves to some degree; *"I'm worthless," "I hate myself," "I'm unloveable."* From the Ho'oponopono perspective they are really just thought-forms arising from the collective subconscious database, tricking us into identifying with them, thinking that the thoughts are who we are at that moment in time. But of course that is not who we really are; our Authentic Self is immortal and at one with Divinity - the source of unconditional love.

But some of these negative thought-forms, and there are probably millions upon millions of them in *the database,* can be really compelling and persistent! The thing is these are your real enemies; the real *inner demons* you need to deal with. So how do you fight these enemies? You don't. Most of the great spiritual teachers throughout the ages have given the same advice: **Love your enemies**. With Ho'oponopono we can do just that. So we begin by taking 100% Responsibility: *"There's something within me that is creating the experience I'm having that I need to let go of."* So that, *"something within me,"* is simply erroneous subconscious thought-forms with which we begin cleaning by practicing Ho'opnopono. In my own experience I suffer from bouts of depression and despair sometimes and can become aware of horrible self loathing

43

thought-forms. What I've found is that you need to make a more regular effort in cleaning these aspects. That's one good reason to practice saying the Ho'oponopono mantra ALL THE TIME, making it become your consistent *internal dialogue.*

Example 5: Body Image

It's well known that many women suffer with painful negative thoughts about the way their body looks and increasingly men. This is probably due, in large part, to some of the powerful marketing strategies used by advertising agencies that manipulate people's subconscious self image conceptions: e.g.) *"Beautiful women are really skinny,"* or, *"Confident, successful men are over 6" tall and have a full head of hair,"* or, *"My ears look really big."* It's true that we are all victim to this manipulation, unless you hide away in a cave, but using Ho'oponopono we can take 100% Responsibility and begin purifying the erroneous thought-forms in *the collective database.*

Projection of The Shadow

The understanding of *the shadow* is one of the unique contributions of Western psychology. The process of denying our own emotions and qualities, good and bad, while projecting them onto other people is technically known as, *"psychodynamic repression."* It's a common experience in everyday life for people to project their so called *shadow aspects of self* onto other people; e.g.) *"It's not me, it's them!"* or, *"I'm OK but I can sense his anger,"* or, *"I can tell they are really judgmental people,"* or, *"she's much more confident than me."* So, basically we can deny aspects within ourself and project and perceive them in others. From the Ho'oponopono perspective all of these *shadow projections* are really just shared subconscious database manifestations - none of it is your Authentic Self. However knowing about *the shadow* can be very useful for our own spiritual development. Let's say we were experiencing difficulty with a *problem person*; using this knowledge we can become aware of our own repressed shadow aspects (subconscious database memories/programs), take Total Responsibility, and then transmute them through Ho'oponopono practice. A classic example would be denying and projecting your own anger onto another person; e.g.) *"He is so angry! He is always getting angry with me and I've done nothing wrong!"* Of course it may well be true that the other person is angry as well but one of the great benefits of taking 100% Responsibility is that everything is taken care of. With Ho'oponopono you acknowledge that there is something within yourself that is co-creating the experience and take on the responsibility of clearing that problem by surrendering to Divinity for transmutation.

The most common form of *shadow projection* is denying negative aspects within ourself and projecting them onto other people. However one of the other things we do is deny our own good qualities and perceive them in others in an exaggerated form; this is what happens with infatuation and obsession. Again from the Ho'oponopono perspective all of these *shadow projections,* positive and negative, are really just shared subconscious database manifestations - none of it is your Authentic Self. So with this practice we can *clean* the *erroneous data* that is causing the *shadow projection*, allowing us to reconnect into our Authentic Self that is connected to the Divine source of unconditional love.

Do you ever find yourself judging people in your everyday life? If so, you can make good use of it, as a spiritual practice, with the knowledge of *shadow projection*. By becoming aware of the judgements you make about other people you can then practice transmuting those thought-forms through the practice of Ho'oponopono. What's beneficial about this particular approach is that it's much easier to spot traits in others, as opposed to oneself, and then take 100% Responsibility: *"What is it within myself that is co-creating the judgement I have of this person?"* Next we would transmute the *erroneous data*, which is *shared data*, within ourself and the other person, through Ho'oponopono practice, bringing us closer to our non-judgemental, loving, Authentic Self.

Relationship Shadow-Work

"Relationship are the Yoga of the West." - Ram Dass

The great thing about knowing about the shadow and our relationships with others, especially intimate relationships, is that they can help us become aware of our own shadow aspects, probably quicker than anything else.

Loving someone authentically and consistently takes courage because inevitably you will have to face your own darkness (fear). The beautiful thing about learning to authentically love someone else, while working through your own shadow aspects (thought-forms), is that you are given the opportunity, with Ho'oponopono, to replace these fear based thought-forms into a connection with your authentic loving self instead, thus enhancing your own lovability.

Common Shadow Aspects In Intimate Relationships

Self Worth: *"I'm not good enough," "They are too good for me."*

Vulnerability: *"I'm too insecure," "I feel too fragile."*

Deservingness: *"I don't deserve to be in a loving relationship," "I don't really deserve to be with him/her."*

Capability: *"I'm incapable of being in a loving relationship,"*

Possibility: *"It's not really possible for me to be in an intimate relationship."*

Competition: *"My partner will probably like him/her better than me because he/she is more xyz."*

"'Practice the wound of love... practice the wound of love.' Real love hurts; real love makes you totally vulnerable and open; real love will take you far beyond yourself; and therefore real love will devastate you. I kept thinking, if love does not shatter you, you do not know love..." - Ken Wilber

The Perceptual Positions

In our minds-eye we can think about situations or events, past, present and future from several different perspectives or points-of-view. The three main *perceptual positions* are explained below:

1st Position (Associated or Self Perspective)

Seeing and hearing the situation through your own eyes and ears. You are primarily aware of your own thoughts and feelings.

2nd Position (Other Person Perspective)

Imagining what it is like to be the other person in the interaction. Imagine stepping into their body, seeing through their eyes, hearing through their ears, feeling their feelings and thinking their thoughts.

3rd Position (Disassociated Perspective, Neutral or Meta Position)

Taking a detached viewpoint. Imagine you are looking at yourself and the other person in the situation, over there. You can try different camera angles to gain new perspectives.

The following method was inspired by, *"The 3-2-1 Shadow Process,"* (Integral Life Practice) and NLP techniques such as the one's I wrote about in one of my previous books, *"The NLP*

Toolbox." Going through the steps below enables you to bring your own shadow aspects to light, transmute them with Ho'oponopono, while developing more empathy and compassion for yourself and the other person. You may well be surprised and delighted at what's revealed with the following method, so give it a go now:

Relationship Shadows Into De-Light

It's best to do this exercise standing up, allowing yourself to physically move location when you are switching into a different Perceptual Position. (Time required: 15/20 minutes.)

1. 1st Position (Associated or Self Perspective)

Notice the person you are having a challenge with in front of you. Describe the qualities that cause you feelings of aversion or attraction. You can let go and express your feelings fully and completely.

2. Imagine talking to this person in front of you, as if they were really there. Express what it is that bothers you about them, such as, *"you are sooo sexy, you are driving me crazy!"* or, *"you are controlling and domineering!"*

Now begin to ask them questions and listen to their responses:

- *"Why are you doing this to me?"*
- *"What do you want from me?"*

- *"What are you trying to show me?"*
- *"What do you have to teach me?"*

Thank them for their feedback.

Notice how you are feeling and ask yourself, *"what do I need to let go of within myself?"* Now practice Ho'oponopono for a few minutes.

3. 2nd Position (Other Person Perspective)

Before switching into 2nd Position, first of all, ask the person in front of you permission to *step into them*. If you get a positive response go ahead and step into their *perceptual position*, otherwise you can just imagine standing next to them instead, looking over their shoulder at yourself.

Stepping In: Imagine stepping into the other person's shoes, becoming them; see through their eyes, hear through their ears, think their thoughts and feel their feelings. Of course from this perspective you will be looking back at yourself. Now, as this person, begin to embody the qualities you identified in Step 1 of this process; e.g.) They annoy you or they drive you crazy with their sexiness. Use *"I statements,"* so you say things such as, *"I drive people crazy with my sexiness,"* or, *"I am really good at annoying people."* Allow yourself to notice how this feels to embody these qualities.

As this person, looking back at *yourself*, answer the question, *"what does that person need to let go of?"*

Remaining in this Perceptual Position, practice

Ho'oponopono for a few minutes.

4. 3rd Position (Disassociated Perspective, Neutral or Meta Position)

So you can see the two of you *"over there."* From this perspective what new insights can you make about the relationship dynamic? You could ask yourself, *"what can I learn from this relationship dynamic?"*

Notice how you are feeling and ask yourself, *"what do I need to let go of within myself?"* Now practice Ho'oponopono for a few minutes.

5. 1st Position (Associated or Self Perspective)

Step back into 1st Position, looking at the person in front of you, and notice any new insights or learnings and ask yourself, *"What is it that I need to let go of within myself?"*

Now practice Ho'oponopono, sitting down if you prefer, for at least 5 minutes; 10 minutes is better.

Top Tip 1: If you feel the need you can repeat the steps going through the Perceptual Positions as many times as you like.

Top Tip 2: As soon as possible meet up with the person, in real life, and notice how things have changed in your perception of the relationship dynamics.

Top Tip 3: Practice this method regularly, making use of a Diary to help you keep on keeping on, so that you will continue enhancing your capacity to love yourself and others more authentically.

How To Keep A Practice Diary

Keeping a record of your Ho'oponopono practice is a very useful endeavour for several reasons:

Encouragement: You can revisit the diary and remember previous successes.

Tracking Your Practice: Keeping track of how many minutes/hours you practiced each day helps you maintain a more consistent practice. Make a goal to practice Ho'oponopono 20, 30, 60 or more minutes every day.

Keep Focussed on Taking 100% Responsibility: Using a diary everyday helps you remember to take 100% Responsibility for the problems that appear in your life.

To keep a diary you can use a traditional paper journal or you can make a simple spreadsheet. You just need to list the date, time practiced with each Ho'oponopono session, the problems you worked on, including any useful insights that you got. That's good enough to help you maintain a more consistent practice.

Practice Reminders

It's really useful to create reminders to help you remember to practice Ho'oponopono regularly. This can be done easily enough using sticky notes or just write *Ho'op!* on a piece of paper and leave it lying around the house, office or car. This is a very simple thing to do and yet it can be very effective in helping you establish the good habit of repeating the Ho'oponopono mantra regularly.

The Art of Blessing

Modern day people have developed very critical minds. We are really good at finding fault with things. Put another way, we could say we are good at cursing things! This attitude doesn't lead to happiness and the antidote is to practice blessing things: You observe a beautiful bird on a tree and you repeat the following phrase again and again like a mantra: *"Thank you", "I love you."* Essentially *blessing* is an exercise that cultivates gratitude.

Gratitude

There is much to be said about a daily practice of Gratitude. Throughout much of our lives, many of us have a tendency to trick ourselves into thinking that we are the victim of circumstance and that what is happening around us should govern our emotions. Deep down we all know that one of the few things we can control in this life is our attitude and learning to practice an, *"attitude of gratitude,"* can improve our lives on many levels. Aside from the obvious shift in your overall mood this practice can bring, there are many theories today that propose that our emotions may have a real, physical effect on our environments. One of the more popular studies on the subject was performed by Doctor Masaru Emoto where he exposed bottles of water to different emotions. He did this by saying things like, *"I love you,"* to one bottle and, *"I hate you,"* to another while focusing on those emotions and then freezing and examining small droplets from each bottle under a microscope. It was found that each emotion produced a different quality of ice crystal. The drops from the, *"I love you,"* bottle formed beautifully coherent and intricate ice crystals while the others showed very little coherence whatsoever. This was repeated with different emotions and it was found that the emotion of gratitude produces the highest coherency in the ice crystals. This suggests that our emotions have a direct effect upon water and possibly other substances as well. Since humans are made up of mostly water, it is only logical that gratitude would affect our biochemistry in the same way.

It feels good to feel grateful and the ability to choose to feel gratitude is the ability to choose your own happiness. It's a good idea to start blessing things as soon as you get up in the morning. Notice the trees, birds, blue sky, sunshine or rain and start blessing them by repeating the mantra, *"I love you,"* *"thank you."* Or how about blessing parts of your body when you shower, then move on to bless your kettle, your coffee cup, your partners hair, the music on the radio and so on. The fact is there are many things to be grateful for and by doing this practice you get your mind into the habit of regularly looking for things to be thankful for and the process gets easier and easier.

I find going for a walk in nature is particularly useful for learning about the art of Blessing. Once upon a time when I was living at the Findhorn Spiritual Community in the north of Scotland I had a wonderful experience one day when walking through the woods. I was feeling quite despondent and so decided to go for a walk and practice Blessing to shift my mood. As I walked along and recited the mantra, *"I love you,"* *"Thank you,"* noticing the beautiful colour of the trees, the sounds of the birds and the fluffy clouds in the sky, I became aware of a dragonfly on a bush. I gently walked towards it and managed to get really close; it was a large male with incredible iridescent blue and green hues. Within moments I was being transcended into that magical state of wonder that only mother nature can instil. And then a female, the brown dragonfly, flew out from nowhere and landed on my shoulder. I've never been so up close to a living, breathing dragonfly. I could clearly see her little face, eyes and mouth while she calmly sat there eating something. Time disappeared directly into the here and now and within that special space she started to clean her face; I had the distinct feeling this beautiful little dragonfly was communicating directly to me: *"Keep cleaning, you are on the right track."* With this experience my entire mood had shifted into wonder, connection and hope.

The Dragonfly - Matsuo Basho

The dragonfly

can't quite land

on that blade of grass.

Love Yourself Loveable In A Nutshell

1. Take 100% Responsibility

With practice you learn to take Total Responsibility for everything that is appearing in your Universe. You accept that you have erroneous *data* arising from your subconscious mind which co-creates the experience you are having, moment by moment.

2. Surrender to Divinity

You realise you don't really know what is going on; life and the Universe is far too vast and complex to understand. You learn to practice letting go of *intellectual ego grasping* and surrender to Divinity to solve your problems.

3. Ho'oponopono Mantra

"I love you"

"I'm sorry"

"Please forgive me"

"Thank you"

You practice saying the four line mantra as often as possible, with the goal of making it your consistent *internal dialogue*.

4. The Art of Blessing

You cultivate a sense of gratitude for all of life by practicing, *"the art of blessing."* You train your mind to see the beautiful and beneficial in all things and bless them again and again with the mantra: *"Thank you", "I love you."*

5. Realising Your Authentic Loving Self

You enjoy the fact that the more you practice this simple yet profound spiritual practice, the more you come to realise your Authentic Loving Self which is connected to the Divine source of unconditional love.

"I wish you peace beyond all understanding."

Appendix

Opening Doors Within

"Love Yourself Loveable" has been the most important and challenging book I've written so far. It was quite a journey. Everyday I read a page from Eileen Caddy's, *"Opening Doors Within,"* and found this an indispensable support guide, with the main message being to connect with your own, *"God within,"* or your own *inner wisdom* or *inner Divinity.* For me this advice works in perfect alignment with the practice of Ho'oponopono. Below I have included three inspiring quotes from, *"Opening Doors Within,"* that seem to complement the themes of this book very nicely.

"Many souls find it very difficult to accept their loving relationship with all human beings. This separation is the cause of all the trouble in the world, the cause of all strife and wars. The place to start putting things right is in yourself and your own personal relationships with all those souls with whom you come into contact. Cease pointing your finger and being critical of those souls with whom you cannot get along in the world. Put your own house in order. You have more than enough to cope with yourself, without tearing your fellow human beings to pieces and pointing out all their faults and failings and where they have gone wrong. When you are willing to face yourself and put things right within, then you will be able to help your fellow human beings simply by your example, not by criticism, intolerance and many words. Love your fellow human beings as I love you. Help them, bless them, encourage them and see the very best in them." - Opening Doors Within, Eileen Caddy

"Do you want to do something to help the world situation? Then look within, for never forget that it all starts in the individual. As you change your consciousness to love, peace, harmony and unity, the consciousness of the whole world will change. But it is not always very pleasant when you start doing it. You will find dark spots which need to be cleared within yourself. You will find that your motives are not always of the highest and that your likes and dislikes are far more pronounced than you imagined. You will find that you are very inclined to discriminate when there should be no discrimination, for all are one in my sight. You will find that your love for one another is not all it should be. Start putting all your cards on the table, and be determined to do something about it, and start doing it now. There is no better time. I am here to help you. Call upon me, and let me guide your every step." - Opening Doors Within, Eileen Caddy

"I was shown the earth like a draught board painted in big black and white squares. As rain came down, the black paint ran into the white, and the whole became a dirty grey. Then even heavier rain came, and the whole was transformed into the purest white. I heard the words:

Have faith. Hold fast and know that the whole earth and all in it are going through a tremendous cleansing process. All is very, very well, for all is going according to my plan. Be at perfect peace." - Opening Doors Within, Eileen Caddy

The 4 Stages of Awakening

The following is a simple model of the stages of awakening

we go through as a human being, taken from Joe Vitale's book, *"At Zero: The Final Secrets to Zero Limits"*

1. Victimhood: This first stage is where most people live. No matter what is happening, it is everyone else's fault or at least someone else's fault. It's the world of the blame game. This is where most people live, as Thoreau pointed out, *"lives of quiet desperation."*

2. Empowerment: *The Secret, The Attractor Factor*, and *Think and Grow Rich* are all about empowerment. It's where you can intend, visualize, and manifest. It's fun - even thrilling. But at some point you run into something you have no control over, often a death or serious illness, and you are faced with limitations. You realize you don't control it all. You can't. This prepares you for the next stage.

3. Surrender: This third stage is the stage of Ho'oponopono as Dr. Hew Len taught it to me. You don't try to run the world. You strive to release your intentions and allow inspirations. You trust a process that is already at work. You learn to tune in to an undercurrent from the Divine. You trust it.

4. Awakening: In this final stage, your ego merges with the Divine mind. Almost nobody gets here, but some do. From the outside, you can't say who is enlightened or not. There's no way for you to know. And it comes by grace. You can't make awakening or enlightenment happen. It's not up to you. All you can do is clean, clear, and prepare. Again, the Law of Attraction isn't dismissed any more than grade school would be to a college student. It's part of your evolution. It's part of the ladder of awakening or, as the late Dr. David Hawkins might have put it, the map of human consciousness. They don't conflict. They are simply on different planes of spirituality.

The following article is from: http://www.mrfire.com/article-archives/new-articles/worlds-most-unusual-therapist.html

The World's Most Unusual Therapist

by Dr. Joe Vitale
www.mrfire.com

Two years ago, I heard about a therapist in Hawaii who cured a complete ward of criminally insane patients--without ever seeing any of them. The psychologist would study an inmate's chart and then look within himself to see how he created that person's illness. As he improved himself, the patient improved.

When I first heard this story, I thought it was an urban legend. How could anyone heal anyone else by healing himself? How could even the best self-improvement master cure the criminally insane?

It didn't make any sense. It wasn't logical, so I dismissed the story.

However, I heard it again a year later. I heard that the therapist had used a Hawaiian healing process called ho'oponopono. I had never heard of it, yet I couldn't let it leave my mind. If the story was at all true, I had to know more.

I had always understood *"total responsibility"* to mean that I am responsible for what I think and do. Beyond that, it's out of my hands. I think that most people think of total responsibility that way. We're responsible for what we do, not what anyone else does. The Hawaiian therapist who healed those mentally ill people would teach me an advanced new perspective about total responsibility.

His name is Dr. Ihaleakala Hew Len. We probably spent an hour talking on our first phone call. I asked him to tell me the complete story of his work as a therapist. He explained that he worked at Hawaii State Hospital for four years. That ward where they kept the criminally insane was dangerous. Psychologists quit on a monthly basis. The staff called in sick a lot or simply quit. People would walk through that ward with their backs against the wall, afraid of being attacked by patients. It was not a pleasant place to live, work, or visit.

Dr. Len told me that he never saw patients. He agreed to have an office and to review their files. While he looked at those files, he would work on himself. As he worked on himself, patients began to heal.

"After a few months, patients that had to be shackled were being allowed to walk freely," he told me. *"Others who had to be heavily medicated were getting off their medications. And those who had no chance of ever being released were being freed."*

I was in awe.

"Not only that," he went on, *"but the staff began to enjoy*

coming to work. Absenteeism and turnover disappeared. We ended up with more staff than we needed because patients were being released, and all the staff was showing up to work. Today, that ward is closed."

This is where I had to ask the million dollar question: *"What were you doing within yourself that caused those people to change?"*

"I was simply healing the part of me that created them," he said.

I didn't understand.

Dr. Len explained that total responsibility for your life means that everything in your life - simply because it is in your life--is your responsibility. In a literal sense the entire world is your creation.

Whew. This is tough to swallow. Being responsible for what I say or do is one thing. Being responsible for what everyone in my life says or does is quite another. Yet, the truth is this: if you take complete responsibility for your life, then everything you see, hear, taste, touch, or in any way experience is your responsibility because it is in your life.

This means that terrorist activity, the president, the economy--anything you experience and don't like--is up for you to heal. They don't exist, in a manner of speaking, except as projections from inside you. The problem isn't with them, it's with you, and to change them, you have to change you.

I know this is tough to grasp, let alone accept or actually live. Blame is far easier than total responsibility, but as I spoke with Dr. Len, I began to realize that healing for him and in ho 'oponopono means loving yourself. If you want to improve your life, you have to heal your life. If you want to cure anyone--even a mentally ill criminal--you do it by healing you.

I asked Dr. Len how he went about healing himself. What was he doing, exactly, when he looked at those patients' files?

"I just kept saying, 'I'm sorry' and 'I love you' over and over again," he explained.

That's it?
That's it.

Turns out that loving yourself is the greatest way to improve yourself, and as you improve yourself, your improve your world. Let me give you a quick example of how this works: one day, someone sent me an email that upset me. In the past I would have handled it by working on my emotional hot buttons or by trying to reason with the person who sent the nasty message. This time, I decided to try Dr. Len's method. I kept silently saying, "I'm sorry" and "I love you," I didn't say it to anyone in particular. I was simply evoking the spirit of love to heal within me what was creating the outer circumstance.

Within an hour I got an e-mail from the same person. He apologized for his previous message. Keep in mind that I didn't take any outward action to get that apology. I didn't even write him back. Yet, by saying "I love you," I somehow healed within me what was creating him.

I later attended a ho 'oponopono workshop run by Dr. Len. He's now 70 years old, considered a grandfatherly shaman, and is somewhat reclusive. He praised my book, The Attractor Factor. He told me that as I improve myself, my book's vibration will raise, and everyone will feel it when they read it. In short, as I improve, my readers will improve.

"What about the books that are already sold and out there?" I asked.

"They aren't out there," he explained, once again blowing my mind with his mystic wisdom. *"They are still in you."*

In short, there is no out there.

It would take a whole book to explain this advanced technique with the depth it deserves. Suffice it to say that whenever you want to improve anything in your life, there's only one place to look: inside you.

"When you look, do it with love."

This article is from the forthcoming book *"Zero Limits"* by Dr. Joe Vitale and Dr. Len

Dr. Joe Vitale is the author of way too many books to list here. His latest title is "The Attractor Factor: 5 Easy Steps for Creating Wealth (or anything else) From the Inside Out." Register for his monthly complimentary ezine at http://www.mrfire.com/

His Executive Mentoring Program is described at http://www.joevitalecoach.com/campaigns/vitale-marketing/index.php

You may forward this in its entirety to anyone you wish.

Hypnotic Marketing Inc.
P.O. Box 2924
Wimberley TX 78676

Member BBB Online 2005

All Therapy is a Form of Manipulation

The following is quite a provocative extract from Cat Saunders interview with Haleakala Hew Len, PhD: *"100% Responsibility and the Possibility of a Hot Fudge Sundae"*

http://www.self-i-dentity-through-hooponopono.com/article5.htm

Cat: Haleakala, when I met you in 1985, I'd just started private practice after working as a counselor in agencies for four years. I remember you said, *"All therapy is a form of manipulation."* I thought, *"Jeez! What am I supposed to do now?"* I knew you were right, so I almost quit! Obviously, I didn't, but that statement completely changed the way I work with people.

Haleakala: Manipulation happens when I (as a therapist) come from the idea that you are ill and I am going to work on you. On the other hand, it's not manipulation if I realize that you are coming to me to give me a chance to look at what's going on in me. There's a big difference.

If therapy is about your belief that you're there to save the other person, heal the other person, or direct the other person, then the information you bring will come out of the intellect, the conscious mind. But the intellect has no real understanding of problems and how to approach them. The intellect is so picayunish is its way of solving problems! It doesn't realize that when a problem is solved by transmutation -- by using Ho'oponopono or related processes -- then the problem and everything related to it is solved, even at microscopic levels and back to the beginning of time.

Recommended Websites

If you want to discover more about Ho'oponopono and become a certified practitioner, I highly recommend Dr. Joe Vitale's, *"Ho'oponopono Practitioner Online Certification Course"*

http://bit.ly/ho-op-cert

Dr. Joe Vitale's Zero Limits Live In Maui DVDs

http://bit.ly/zerolimitsdvds

Other Websites of Interest

http://zero-wise.com

http://www.self-i-dentity-through-hooponopono.com

http://www.morrnahsprayer.com

http://www.mabelkatz.com

My Ho'oponopono Practitioner Certificate

Global Sciences Foundation

www.myglobalsciencesfoundation.org

This is to certify that _____ Mr. Colin Smith _____ having satisfactorily completed the required studies, has been found by the Board of Directors to possess the qualifications required by Constitutional bylaws, and is hereby registered as a

Certified Ho'oponopono Practitioner

In Witness Whereof, the Signature of the Administration is hereunto affixed on this __21st__ day of __October__ , __2016__ .

Certificate No. __1045__

Dr. Joe Vitale
Ho'oponopono Instructor

Mathew Dixon
Ho'oponopono Instructor

Bibliography

Bibliography

Zero Limits: The Secret Hawaiian System For Wealth, Health, Peace & More - Joe Vitale & Ihaleakala Hew Len

At Zero: The Quest For Miracles Through Ho'oponopono - Joe Vitale

How To Become A Miracle Worker With Your Life - Dr. Bruno R. Cignacco

The Easiest Way - Mabel Katz

Integral Spirituality - Ken Wilber

Integral Psychology - Ken Wilber

Four Steps To Forgiveness - William Fergus Martin

Escape From The Matrix: Pathways To Liberation - Zivorad Mihajlovic Slavinski

Return To Oneness: Principles And Practice Of Spiritual Technology - Zivorad Mihajlovic Slavinski

Transcendance - Zivorad Mihajlovic Slavinski

Opening Doors Within - Eileen Caddy

Journey of Souls - Michael Newton

Eros Unredeemed - Dieter Duhm

The Truth: An Uncomfortable Book About Relationships - Neil Strauss

Sex At Dawn: How We Mate, Why We Stray, And What It Means For Modern Relationships - Christopher Ryan & Cecilda Jetha

Deepening Love, Sex & Intimacy: A True Story - Graham Meltzer

Psychic Sexuality - The Bio-Psychic "Anatomy" Of Sexual Energies - Ingo Swann

Integral Protocol: How To Integrate Internal Conflicts - Vladimir Stojakovic